Not guilty

NOT GUILTY

An abridged version, rewritten for today's readers, of
the classic *Justification* by James Buchanan, D.D., LI.D,
first publishd in 1867. (The full version is available
from the Banner of Truth Trust).

Prepared by John Appleby
with a foreword by Herbert M. Carson

Joint Managing Editors:
J. P. Arthur M.A.
H. J. Appleby

© GRACE PUBLICATIONS TRUST
139 Grosvenor Avenue
London, N5 2NH,
England

First published 1990
2nd Impression 1995

British Library Cataloguing in Publication Data
Appleby, John
Not Guilty
1. Christian doctrine. Justification
I. Title II. Buchanan, James. Doctrine of justification
234.7

ISBN 0 946462 22 4

Distributed by: EVANGELICAL PRESS
12 Wooler Street
Darlington
Co. Durham DL1 1RQ
England

Printed in Great Britain by
Cox & Wyman Ltd, Reading.

Cover design: L. L. Evans

'I have myself taught for twenty years the doctrine of faith alone by which, embracing the merits of Christ, we stand accepted before the tribunal of God; and yet the old and tenacious mire clings to me so that I find myself wanting to come to God bringing something in my hand, for which he should bestow his grace upon me. I cannot attain to casting myself on pure and simple grace only, and yet this is highly necessary'.

Martin Luther
(From Scott's *Continuation of Milner's History*, vol. i, p.42)

Contents

Part II: Explanation of the doctrine

Foreword

Are the Christian churches in Britain and the Western World in a healthy condition at the present time? Only someone totally blind to the situation would cheerfully say 'Yes'. With falling membership, waning missionary concern, interest in religious excitement rather than in godliness and evangelism, the verdict must be a negative one, qualified only by the fact that there are many notable exceptions to the general malaise.

If we try to analyse why there is such weakness the answer will be seen, at least partly, in Martin Luther's celebrated saying that the doctrine of justification by faith is the test of a standing or falling church, that is, of a healthy or a sick church. Judging by the neglect of this basic doctrine (and in many cases the ignorance of it) we need hardly be surprised that the churches so often display weakness rather than strength. Indeed what seems sometimes to be vigorous strength turns out to be a frantic state of frenzy rather than of purposeful activity.

Is it really true however that this doctrine is either neglected or seemingly misunderstood? The answer to that question may be seen in quite a lot of evangelistic preaching; sinners are urged to turn in repentance from their sins and urged to trust in Christ alone. So far so good — but what is promised to the penitent? Forgiveness of sins and new life — these constitute the usual answer. Yet judged by the New Testament this is an inadequate answer since pardon is not the same as justification, and a new pattern of life according to Romans 5-8 emerges from justification.

The situation is even worse when the gospel is being presented to children. Often they are urged to love the Lord Jesus. Yet the command of Scripture to love the Lord with all our hearts is the summary of the first part of the law. But law, as Paul pointed out in the first three chapters of Romans, brings not salvation but a realization of our sin and our guilt. Indeed love for God and for the Christ who died for us is seen in Romans 5:5 as among the *consequences* of justification by faith. In Galatians 5:22 love is one element in the *fruit* of the Spirit.

Yet it is not only in the area of evangelism and teaching that neglect of justification by faith is so apparent. The neglect is seen also in the quality of Christian life — what used to be referred to as godliness! Handley Moule of Durham (1841-1920) added a further comment to Luther's dictum by saying that the doctrine of justification was not only the mark of a standing or falling church but also of a standing or a falling soul! It was an apt addition. Judged by New Testament standards a man or woman only has a healthy beginning to the Christian life when they have grasped in some measure what it means to be justified by faith.

Furthermore, growth in godliness is not a religious duty but a grateful response to God's grace. It is justification which is the nerve centre of such gratitude. Furthermore if the Christian is to continue in the face of much hostility and much discouragement — indeed even when there is personal failure — there must be a strong conviction of final perseverance. Once again it is a firm grasp of justification which will give such solid assurance.

When Buchanan wrote his great book on justification — and its republication first in full and now in abbreviated form indicates its continuing value — he did not face a debate which has come into prominence today; namely, the ecumenical discussion on church reunion. In his day Rome's rejection of Luther's and the reformation view was accepted both by Rome and by Protestants as a clear-cut issue. Today however, with the pressure for reunion between Anglicans and Rome, the issue of justification has re-surfaced as a crucial issue. The world-famous Hans Kung (writing before he was deprived by the pope of his status as a Roman Catholic theologian) produced a major book on the subject. The American Roman Catholics and Lutherans have discussed it and produced a massive report. More recently the Anglican Roman Catholic International Commission (ARCIC for short!) has issued its report on salvation. So the issue is top of the agenda. It is a timely moment for a wider readership to sample the masterly exposition by Buchanan.

If then we view the doctrine of justification by faith as being basic to the individual Christian, vital to the church and vital also to the relationship between churches — from this starting point we move on to discover what this doctrine really means. Clearly our guide in this must be Scripture and this means that the context for all our study is the biblical stress on *the priority of the grace of God*. God took the initiative in creation. He has also taken the first step in the work of salvation. Our exposition of any doctrine in the Bible must be firmly rooted in the underlying conviction that we are — without any condition or qualification — totally in debt to God's grace. Paul puts it succinctly and very personally: 'By the grace of God I am what I am' (1 Cor. 15:10).

This rules out any notion of human merit. We cannot earn God's favour. We cannot produce any merit of our own. God will never be in debt to us and thus compelled to reward us. We will always, at every stage, be in debt to him. Paul emphasizes this point, and gives the reason for it in Ephesians 2:8-9: 'For it is by grace you have been saved through faith — and this not from yourselves, it is the gift of God — not by works, so that no one can boast'.

This means that the faith of the justified one must never be seen as the sinner's contribution. Justification is not the reward for our meritorious faith. Rather it is a case of faith being itself a gift from God. Faith is the empty hand stretched out to receive the gift. Indeed an even better illustration is the miracle of the healing of the man with the withered hand. He needed the supernatural power of Christ to enable him to respond to the Lord's command to stretch out his hitherto useless hand (Matt. 12:10-13).

One of the major doctrinal statements of the

Protestant Reformation was the Thirty Nine Articles of the Church of England. There was a Latin version of these articles and in the article on Justification a subtle use of two Latin prepositions highlighted the fact that justification is not earned. The two words were *propter* meaning 'on account of' and *per* meaning simply 'through'. The articles taught that we are justified 'on account of' the merits of Christ 'through' (i.e. by means of) faith. So there can never be any grounds for self-congratulation. If we have responded in faith then it has been a similar response to Lydia's at Philippi — 'The Lord opened her heart to respond to Paul's message' (Acts 16:14). Such faith emerges out of repentance as we become aware of our sinfulness. Yet once again, in our repentance, it is God to whom we owe a debt of gratitude that we have turned from sin. Peter noted in his preaching that both repentance and forgiveness were God's gracious gifts — 'God exalted him (i.e. Christ)... that he might give repentance and forgiveness to Israel' (Acts 5:31). Peter's report to his critics in Jerusalem stressed the same truth and elicited from them the grateful acknowledgement: 'So then God has even granted to the Gentiles repentance unto life' (Acts 11:18).

Faith thus is not what Luther's opponents maintained; namely, a mental acceptance of the dogmatic teaching of the church. He emphasized instead that it was the response of the heart issuing in simple reliance on Christ. The reply of God to such simple faith is to justify the sinner. At this mention of justification the gap between Luther and Rome is seen as being even wider. It still yawns widely today! The core of the

13

disagreement lies in the meaning of the word 'to justify'. Does it mean to 'make righteous' as Rome taught or 'to declare righteous' as Luther maintained and indeed as Paul had maintained in the letters to the Romans and to the Galatians.

Lest someone complains that this is a typical theologian's wrangle about petty details, it is important to stress how deeply significant the issue is. It has a direct bearing on the question of assurance — may I say with confidence: 'I know I am saved and going to heaven' or merely 'I hope I am going to heaven'? Clearly the New Testament not only teaches a firm assurance but exhibits men and women who display such joyful confidence.

If Rome is right and justification means making the sinner righteous,then the ground of our assurance is the extent and the durability of our own inner righteousness. To the Christian, aware of indwelling sin and sadly aware of sinful failure, this is a very shaky basis for assurance. It comes therefore as no surprise that the counter-Reformation Council of Trent taught that 'no one can know with infallible certainty of faith that he has received the grace of God'(Session 6, Chap. 9). The issue, in short, is whether justification has to do with our essential character or with our new standing before God. Are we accepted because we are working to improve the goodness infused into us by baptism, or are we recognised as righteous while still evidently sinful? The Bible clearly supports Luther's dictum that the Christian is 'At the same time justified and a sinner'.

The grounds of our acceptance are not our inherent righteousness but rather the righteousness of Christ which God graciously sets to our account when we trust in the Saviour. It was when Luther was studying and teaching the Letter to the Romans that 'the light dawned' and he saw the point. Clearly a righteous God requires righteousness. Such righteousness is indeed beyond our reach because of our sin. However God exhibits a perfect righteousness in his Son and it is the righteousness on which we rest all our confidence.

All this leads to a further and even more basic question — what does the Bible then mean by righteousness? The answer to that is seen in the title given to the Saviour. He is 'Jesus Christ the Righteous One' (1 John 2:1). He is such because he always did in his earthly ministry and also does eternally in his heavenly ministry, what is pleasing in every respect to the Father. Human beings by contrast are unrighteous because we fail to do God's will and in addition we do what is not God's will. There are sins of omission and sins of commission and these are merely symptoms of the underlying fact of our fallen nature and our essentially unrightous character.

What is it then which conveys to us not only the knowledge of what God requires but also of our sinful failure? The answer, as Paul shared in Romans, is to be found in God's law. That law is written on the conscience of every human being and spelled out in explicit details in the Scriptures. This means that righteousness basically means keeping God's law, and unrighteousness is breaking God's law. That is why the consequences of law-breaking are so serious in that God's wrath is declared in judgment and condemnation.

Yet there is one and only one example of a perfect

human righteousness. It is in the man Christ Jesus. He could say — and only he could say it: 'I have come to do your will, O God' (Heb. 10:7, cf. Psalm 40:6-8).

If however all were given by Christ was an example of perfect righteousness we would be plunged into despair by our inability to reach such a standard. The gospel however neither tantalises nor mocks us with a standard impossible to reach. This righteousness rather is set to our account just as our sin was set to his, as Paul pointed out in 2 Cor. 5:21 'God made him who had no sin to be sin for us, so that in him we might become the righteousness of God'.

In order to appreciate the full riches of justification it is helpful to view Christ's righteousness from two directions. On one side he is the great sin-bearer who took the guilt of law-breakers upon himself and bore the penalty which divine justice demanded. He is the one who himself bore our sins in his body on the tree (1 Pet. 2:24). Hence there is deliverance from guilt, and freedom from condemnation. Viewed from another aspect he is not only the one who stood as the divine substitute in the place of law-breakers, he is, as our representative, the perfect law-keeper. His keeping of the law was not only in letter but in motive and in spirit. It is this positive righteousness which is set to our account. Thus we are not only freed from the guilt of law-breaking but we are viewed as law-keepers because of our faith in Christ.

The oft-quoted reply of the Sunday school pupil was only partially correct when the child said that to be justified meant to be treated 'just as if I'd never sinned'. As forgiven sinners we rejoice in that truth even if we are averse to puns! But justifications means *even more*.

16

It is also just as if I'd always perfectly kept God's law. I am not only pardoned but fully accepted.

It was the realization of the rich fulness of justification which gave Paul such a joyful confidence and impelled him into a passionate devotion to Christ and also an urgency to make this good news known. It was the same experience of forgiveness knit to God's gracious acceptance of the justified sinner which not only banished Luther's anguished doubts but made him ready to challenge the might of pope and emperor. It is the same message which will still stir forgiven sinners to grateful obedience and will still set churches on a constructive path of biblical worship and witness.

Herbert M. Carson
Leicester
1990

Preface

It is God, our Maker and Judge, to whom we need to relate. Clearly, any wrong understanding as to how to be acceptable to him must have serious consequences. It would be tragic to journey through life and not arrive at the expected end! How important for us, then, to know what is the right way to be justified in God's sight.

The way of justification, to be of help to us, must take account of three facts: that we are helpless in God's sight; that a holy God cannot simply overlook our sin; that Jesus Christ graciously made himself a substitute for sinners — their sin for him, his obedience and holiness for them. And these facts are stated on the authority of the Bible, God's revelation of truth to us.

Where such Bible truth is ignored, or misunderstood, there will follow a wrong view of how to be acceptable to God. The true knowledge of salvation is lost if the truth about justification is lost.

In this book Dr Buchanan seeks to explain what the Bible teaches about justification. It is doubtful whether any other book has presented the subject so fully.

H. J. Appleby

Introduction

Just as scientists continually make new discoveries about the nature of the universe, so the study of the Scriptures can result in a new understanding of its truths. Therefore, even though the doctrine of justification was so well defined by Luther at the time of the Reformation, there is good reason for a fresh look at the truth.

Moreover, the doctrine will be new to each new generation of believers; and it will be new to many who call themselves Christians but who, for various reasons, may not previously have experienced the meaning of this truth personally.

Further, to understand the doctrine of justification is the best defence against two common errors in our society today. On the one hand, there are many who argue that they will believe only what they can prove by human reason — rationalists. On the other hand, there are many who feel satisfaction only in the performance of religious ceremonies and religious duties—ritualists.

The rationalist is in error because he is ignorant of, or unwilling to believe, the demands of God upon him. The ritualist, by supposing that his ceremonies are adequate to please God, is in error because he has no proper sense of his own sin and guilt, nor of the excellence of what Christ has done for sinners.

The Bible teaching about justification by faith includes: the study of God's holy and unalterable demands upon us all; the study of our inexcusable guilt in God's sight; the study of the glorious salvation procured by Jesus Christ which fully satisfies God's justice on behalf of sinners. To understand justification, therefore, is to escape the errors of both the rationalist and the ritualist, so common all around us.

It should be noted that although the biblical doctrine of justification was distinctively taught in the Reformation, it was not entirely unknown before then. The truth is found in the Old and New Testaments and can be found in the writings of many of the early church fathers.

Even from as early as the second century AD there have been those who have attacked this doctrine as not being a Bible truth. And we must never forget that the unbelief so deeply rooted in all human hearts disputes the need for the justification of which the Bible speaks.

All these things make the study of this truth very needful for us.

Dr James Buchanan
1867

Part I: The history of this doctrine

Lecture 1: Justification as found in the Old Testament Scriptures

In these lectures, 'justification' means that a person is regarded and treated by God as free from all wrongdoing and as possessing perfect holiness. Such a person enjoys God's favour and blessing. Justification means more than mere pardon for sin; it means that the justified person is regarded as having kept all God's laws perfectly.

God's laws are the only rules by which we can be either justified or condemned. Surely, therefore, we must say that justification is not possible for us, for we have all broken those laws. How shall we ever be justified? This is the subject of our book. The gospel of Jesus Christ is able to solve the problem.

The Bible describes two methods of justification.

i. There was a time when a man and a woman lived free from all wrongdoing. I refer to our first parents, Adam and Eve. They were created holy and happy and free from any sin. God revealed to them that, by keeping his commands, they could remain in that holy, happy state, justified by their obedience. Disobedience, God said, would result in the loss of divine favour and in their death.

The first method of justification was by obedience to God's command. But this method was only suitable for those people who were already holy and sinless. No sooner had Adam and Eve disobeyed God than this method of justification could help them no more. God's law, broken by their disobedience, must condemn them as law-breakers: it could not justify them; i.e. it could not declare them holy and free from wrongdoing.

ii. From the time that Adam and Eve fell into sin by their disobedience, it has been necessary for justification to be possible for those who are already sinners. *A second method of justification* was revealed by God when Adam and Eve were summoned to appear before him (Genesis 3:14-16). The words God spoke to them then meant that he was taking their justification into his own hands; that he would send to earth a Saviour, born of a woman, who would rescue sinners from Satan's grasp.

This first announcement of God's merciful purpose was made in very general terms. Yet it contained the same truths expressed so fully in the New Testament gospel. It was a method of justification *by God's grace*. A divine deliverer was to come — Jesus Christ — who would suffer for sin in the place of sinners. God has *sovereignly* taken over the justifying of helpless sinners by his gracious gift of salvation.

Because of God's promise of a Saviour, Adam and Eve, and subsequent Old Testament believers, were aware of mixed feelings: on the one hand there was a dread of God because of their disobedience to him; and on the other hand there was hope in God's promise of their deliverance. These feelings were expressed by the rite of animal sacrifices offered to God.[1]

An animal was slain. Its life-blood was shed. That expressed the truth of God's wrath in judgment. The animal was innocent, and yet was killed as *a substitute for the sinner*. That expressed the truth of a divine deliverer being provided.

Such Old Testament sacrifices obviously described in symbolic form the work of Jesus Christ— 'the Lamb of God' who would take away sin (John 1:29). By offering such a sacrifice and believing what it signified, Abel 'obtained witness that he was righteous' (Hebrews 11:4). Clearly, in those times — as now — all believers in God's way of salvation by the death of an innocent substitute were — and are — justified. Unbelievers who reject God's way of salvation must remain under the judgment of God for their sin.

In the flood which destroyed everyone except Noah and his family (Genesis 7:23), God demonstrated both his wrath on the sinners who clung to their unbelief and his justification of those obedient believers in the ark.

After the flood the revelation of the method of

justification by God mercifully providing the Saviour became increasingly clear. The most memorable case of this justification by grace in patriarchal times was that of Abraham. His case is often used in the New Testament writings as an example of this second method of justification (John 8:56; Romans 4:3; Galatians 3:6; James 2:23).

The next great era in the history of justification in the Old Testament was that introduced by the giving of the law to Moses at Sinai. The purpose of this law was two-fold — to govern the life of the Jewish nation and to educate them to be ready for the promised Saviour through whom, as Abraham understood, 'all the families of the earth would be blessed' (Genesis 22:18).

In its relation to the first of these purposes — the law as a guide to national life — the physical welfare of the nation depended on their obedience to it. In this national sense, their prosperity depended on their deeds. The law could be thought of as a national 'covenant of works'.

As far as the eternal salvation of believers is concerned, the second purpose of the law was to convict of sin and so educate the Jews in preparation for the coming of the Saviour. The apostle Paul used the law in this way, to prove the impossibility of anyone being justified by keeping the law, for it could not be kept perfectly by sinful creatures.

The law, then, was not contrary to the method of justification in which God graciously provided a Saviour. Instead, the law was designed to contribute to the knowledge of that method. All the legal ceremonies commanded to be observed were meaningful symbols of spiritual things. The whole ritual of the Old Testament church illustrated different aspects of the work of Christ the Saviour. So the devout Israelite, looking forward, was justified by grace through faith in Christ no less than the Christian believer of New Testament days who looks back.

During the period of the law, God sent the Jews a succession of prophets to explain both the national and the spiritual significance of his law. In the time of David and Samuel there was a great increase in the knowledge revealed about the coming Messiah. Afterwards, Isaiah and other prophets described him in great detail. These truths were the basis of the faith of the true believers of the Jewish church.

In the opening pages of Matthew and Luke in the New Testament we find mention of several true believers who looked for justification by God's fulfilment of his promise, given long before, to send a Saviour. Zacharias, Elizabeth, Simeon, Anna and others 'looked for redemption in Jerusalem' (Luke, chapters 1 and 2).

The Old Testament, considered as a record of knowledge of spiritual life, has no parallel in any other ancient philosophical writers. The Old Testament is full of the gospel truth that God gives justification freely to sinners who believe in him. Only because this gospel was known and believed in the Old Testament days could the apostles base so much of their teaching about this method of justification on the experiences of Abraham and

David (Romans, chapter 4) and other Old Testament believers (Hebrews, chapter 11).

Notes

[1] It seems extremely likely that animal sacrifice was an institution of God, not a human invention. Abel offered 'by faith' (Hebrews 11:4), i.e. believingly. He must, therefore, have had some divine authority as the reason for his action. Belief implies something to be believed: in this case, a divine instruction to offer sacrifices.

Lecture 2: Justification as found in the New Testament Scriptures

We turn our attention now to what was thought about the doctrine of justification among Gentiles and Jews when the gospel was first brought to them.

We have already seen that from the beginning of history the divine teaching on justification for sinners included the promise of a Saviour to come and instruction about the practice of sacrifice. From Adam to Abraham these things were universally known. There was then no division in the world between Gentile and Jew. The situation after Abraham was different:

i. *Among the Gentiles*. The knowledge of the truth was forgotten or distorted by those who received no further revelation from God such as was given to Abram and the Jews. The Gentile world retained some ideas of primitive religious worship. Animal sacrifice continued. But it was all without the knowledge of gospel truth and consequently developed into systems of heathen superstition. Yet the sad earnestness of heathen worship can be impressive. It demonstrates the fact that people sensed a need to be somehow accepted by a supreme power, though they had only a very defective knowledge of God, of sin, and of the need of salvation.

The educated Gentiles, scorning superstition, sought by philosophy to find answers to their religious questions. In the dim light of the revelation of God in nature, they sought to grapple with their problems. They had no definite doctrine of justification. Sometimes, indeed, they argued that human beings were virtuous enough in themselves and that it was quite wrong to regard them as helpless sinners needing justification.

ii. *Among the Jews.* The truth of justification by God's grace through faith was never entirely lost. Yet it was obscured by wrong teaching. Paul described the leaders of the Jews as 'ignorant of God's righteousness and going about to establish their own righteousness' (Romans 10:3). The error of many Jews, therefore, was that of self-righteousness. They thought that people, by their own suffering, could obtain forgiveness for their sins; and that by their good deeds (prayer, almsgiving, religious ceremony, belief in the law) they could merit eternal life.[1] This teaching showed a lack of knowledge of the true nature of sin and a disregard for all that Jesus Christ did to *procure* salvation for sinners.

Thus, Gentiles and Jews alike came to believe that what they had done, or might thereafter do, could justify them; and so they both put their trust in the *outward* observance of religious ceremonies to satisfy God. The gospel of salvation by God's grace was preached to people who believed these Gentile and Jewish errors. Appreciating this fact helps us to understand many parts of the Gospels and Epistles. Our Lord, in expounding the spiritual meaning of God's law, stresses the requirement of *inward* obedience of the heart and mind. He insists on the fact of everlasting punishment for sin and on the necessity for an inward new birth. We even find him using the law in its national covenant sense to provoke a sense of conviction for sin — 'Do this and you will live' (Luke 10:28). Our Lord seeks to prepare the way for the gospel of justification by faith alone (John 3:16).

The apostles dealt in similar manner with the same errors of Gentile and Jew. Paul repeatedly showed that both Gentile and Jew were sinners, helpless under the holy wrath of God, who could not by their own deeds obtain any acceptance with God. Thus Paul proved the urgent need for a method of justification other than that which people could themselves devise. The way was prepared for the 'righteousness of God which is by faith alone' (Romans 3:22).

It is instructive to realise that these errors of Gentiles and Jews are the same errors which the church still has to combat in teaching the biblical doctrine of justification. All other religions have this in common; all teach some form of human self-sufficiency and are more or less opposed to an entire dependence on the grace of God for justification. In the case of the Jews there was the additional error that they relied for justification on their special privilege as God's chosen nation. All three of these errors can be found among many nominal adherents of Christianity today.

iii. In addition to the errors that were present when the New Testament gospel was first preached, there arose in the early Christian church further questions about justification. These originated in the influence of Judaism and of Greek philosophy.

From Jewish influences came the questions: 'Should Jewish Christians continue to observe the ceremonies of Judaism?' 'Should Gentiles wishing to become Christians first ceremonially become Jews?' 'Is faith in Christ enough for a sinner's pardon and acceptance with God, without obedience to the moral or ceremonial law as the reason for justification (Acts 15)?'

The purpose of the letter to the Hebrews was to persuade Jewish believers that, as Christians, they now had the reality of which Judaism contained only the symbols. The record in Acts of the Holy Spirit's coming in fulness on Gentile believers made it clear that Jewish ceremonies were not essential to Christian experience. The letters to the Romans and the Galatians insist that salvation is by faith in Christ alone and does not need any human good deed to make it effective. A study of how the apostles dealt with the questions of their day gives us much information as to how they understood the doctrine of justification.

From Greek philosophical influence came the heresy that all material substance is essentially evil. Our physical bodies were therefore said to be inherently sinful. This led to a denial of the true fleshly nature of the Lord's body, so that Christ who suffered and shed his blood was not capable of being a true substitute for sinners. In that case, justification was no longer possible by faith in Christ as Saviour. Against such error, the aged apostle John earnestly asserted: 'Every spirit that acknowledges that Jesus Christ has come *in the flesh* is from God, but every spirit that does not acknowledge Jesus has come in the flesh is not from God' (1 John 4:1-3). It is still true that the corruption of Christian truth often arises from the influence of 'philosophy and empty deception' (Colossians 2:8).

Notes

[1] Nominal Christians sometimes suppose that their good deeds can be set over against their sins to balance them, making those people 'neutral'. In this way, sin need not be atoned for. But self-righteous Jews never dared to think that sin could *escape* punishment. They knew that their sins must be fully paid for and thought that eternal life could then be worked for. Their error was to suppose that those who are sinners can nevertheless pay for their sins and then live sinlessly to earn eternal life.

Lecture 3: Justification as taught by the church fathers to AD1200

The writings of the church fathers are not inspired Scripture. We do not look to them as authoritative for teaching. But they do provide evidence of teaching that was given in the church of their day. We possess an unbroken chain of writings from the time of the apostles until today which can show us the whole history of Christian thought on the subject of justification.

The question we are asking the early church fathers is: 'Can the doctrine of justification by grace through faith in the merits of Christ be traced in some of the writings throughout the first period of the church's history?' It it is so, then we will have conclusive proof that the doctrine was not an invention of Luther, as is sometimes said! But if the truth was known to any of the early fathers, then it was certainly known before the Reformation.

Clement of Rome (perhaps referred to in Philippians 4:3) says in his letter to the Corinthians:

'We also, being called through his (God's) will in Christ Jesus, are not justified through ourselves, neither through our own wisdom or understanding, or piety, or works which we have done in holiness of heart, but through faith...'

(Epistle to Corinthians)

Ignatius, a disciple of the apostle John, wrote:

'His (Christ's) cross, and his death, and his resurrection, and the faith which is through him, are my unpolluted muniments[1]; and in these, through your prayers, I am willing to have been justified.'

(Epistle to Philadelphians)

Polycarp (died AD155), also a disciple of the apostle John, wrote:

'I know that through grace you are saved, not of works, but by the will of God, through Jesus Christ.'

(Epistle to Philippians)

Justin Martyr (died AD165) wrote:

'No longer by the blood of goats and of sheep, or by the ashes of a heifer... are sins purged[2]; but by faith, through the blood of Christ and his death, who died on this very account.'

(Dialogue with Trypha)

In a letter (written about AD 150) addressed to a person

called Diognetus, who seemed to be enquiring about Christianity, there are the following sentences:

> 'God gave his own Son the ransom for us ... for what, save his righteousness, could cover our sins? In whom was it possible that we, transgressors and ungodly as we were, could be justified, save in the Son of God alone?... O unexpected benefit, that the transgression of many should be hidden in one righteous Person and that the righteousness of One should justify many transgressors.'

In the period beginning with the reign of Emperor Constantine (died AD337) when Christianity became an officially recognized religion, as distinct from a persecuted faith, a number of heresies arose in regard to several basic Christian doctrines. Inevitably, error concerning one Christian truth involved error concerning others also: e.g. defective views of sin prevented some from understanding their need of a Saviour. Other heresies related to the Trinity, the incarnation of Christ, the inability of a lost sinner to perform spiritual actions. These errors all weakened the understanding of biblical justification.

In combating these heresies and re-affirming the sinful impotence of the human nature, the necessity of salvation by grace and the real atonement offered by Christ, the faithful few of the church laid secure foundations for the doctrine of justification by grace through faith in Christ.

Irenaeus (died early third century), a disciple of Polycarp wrote:

'...through the obedience of one man who first was born from the Virgin, many should be justified and receive salvation.'

Cyprian (died AD258), a bishop in the church in North Africa, wrote:

'If Abraham believed in God and it was imputed to him for righteousness, then each one, who believes in God and lives by faith, is found to be a righteous person.'

Athanasius, bishop of Alexandria for forty-six years (died AD373), wrote:

'Not by these (i.e. human efforts) but by faith, a man is justified as was Abraham.'

Basil, bishop of Cappadocia (died AD379) was a prolific writer and has left us words such as these:

'This is the true and perfect glorying in God, when a man is not lifted up on account of his own righteousness, but has known himself to be wanting in true righteousness and to be justified by faith alone in Christ.'

Ambrose, bishop of Milan (died AD397), famous as a great preacher, has left us these words:

'Without the works of the law, to an ungodly man, that is to say, a Gentile, believing in Christ, his "faith

39

is imputed for righteousness" as also it was to Abraham.'

From **Origen,** a great Christian teacher, thinker and writer (died AD253) comes the following:

'Through faith, without the works of the law, the dying thief was justified; because ... the Lord inquired not what he had previously wrought, nor yet waited for his performance of some work after he should have believed; but ... he took him unto himself for a companion, justified through his confession alone.'

Jerome, the great translator of the Bible into Latin (died AD420), has written:

'When an ungodly man is converted, God justifies him through faith alone, not on account of good works which he possessed not.'

Chrysostom, perhaps the greatest preacher among all the church fathers (died AD407) spent many years in Constantinople. From him we have:

'What then did God do? He made (says Paul) a righteous Person (Christ) to be a sinner[3], in order that he might make sinners righteous ... it is the righteousness of God, when we are justified, not by works... but by grace, where all sin is made to vanish away.'

From **Augustine,** the bishop of Hippo near Carthage, a

40

great expounder of the theology of salvation by God's grace alone (died AD430), we have:

'Grace is given to you, not wages paid to you... it is called grace because it is given gratuitously. By no precedent (previous) merits did you buy what you have received. The sinner therefore received this grace first, that his sins should be forgiven him... good works follow after a justified person; they do not go before in order that he may be justified... good works, following after justification, show what a man has received.'

Anselm of Canterbury (died AD1109), a great theologian, perhaps best known for his study of Christ's atonement for sin, wrote:

'Do you believe that you cannot be saved but by the death of Christ? Go, then, and ... put all your confidence in this death alone. If God shall say to you, "You are a sinner", say to him, "I place the death of our Lord Jesus Christ between me and my sin".'

From **Bernard of Clairvaux,** reckoned to be the last of the church fathers (died AD1153) comes the following:

'Shall not all our righteousness turn out to be mere unrighteousness and deficiency? What, then, shall it be concerning our sins, when not even our righteousness can answer for itself? Wherefore... let us flee, with all humility to Mercy which alone can save our souls... whosoever hungers and thirsts after righteousness, let him believe in thee, who "justifies the ungodly"; and thus, being justified by faith alone, he shall have peace with God.'[4]

Thus we see that, beyond all doubt, the doctrine of justification by grace through faith was not a novelty introduced into the church by Luther and Calvin. Though there were many heresies and much corrupt understanding through the first centuries of the church's history, there was also a continual stream of the greatest writers and thinkers who held and taught this biblical truth.

Notes

[1]'Muniments' = title deeds, documents giving evidence of legal ownership of something — Editor.

[2]The reference is presumably to Hebrews 10:11 — Editor.

[3]The reference is presumably to 2 Corinthians 5:21. In fact Chrysostom says more than Scripture. Christ was never made a sinner — Editor.

[4]Archbishop Ussher (1581-1656) collected quotations from twenty-eight early church fathers, showing that in every century down to the twelfth there were those who held the biblical doctrine of justification. (Ussher, *Answers to a Jesuit's Challenge*, pages 472-505).

Footnote to Lecture 3

In the original form of this lecture, Buchanan spends some time explaining that when Augustine used the verb 'to merit' (appearing to mean that sinners could themselves earn [deserve] their justification) he often meant no more than that they could 'obtain' justification. Buchanan argues that in Augustine's day the Latin verb meaning 'to merit' was sometimes used simply to mean 'to gain, or obtain'. Nowadays, says Buchanan, 'when the meaning of the term has been entirely changed, it is not safe to speak of merits at all.'

It is obviously quite unbelievable that Augustine, who so strongly championed the truth of salvation by God's grace alone, would at the same time teach that justification could be earned by human effort! A whole section of the lecture is therefore omitted from this abridgement as no longer relevant — Editor.

Lecture 4: Justification as taught at the time of the Protestant Reformation

The re-discovery of the doctrine of justification was the reason for the sixteenth century Reformation. The Reformation was a reaction against the false doctrines and corrupt practices that had developed in the Roman Catholic Church before that time. Let us trace how these errors gradually developed.

First, there was the Roman Catholic teaching concerning pardon for sin. It was taught that all sin (including original sin[1]) done before the baptism was pardoned by baptism and that through baptism the person actually received new spiritual life.

All sin committed after baptism was pardoned only by confession to the priest, fulfilment of penances[2] and personal suffering in purgatory[3]. (This is not really a pardon at all because sinners are not freely forgiven but have a long process of suffering to endure).

Sin was divided by Roman Catholics into two types, *mortal* — which only Christ's death could atone for, and *venial* — deserving only the punishment of penances in this life. (The Bible makes no such distinction but regards every sin as 'mortal').

Justification, according to these teachings, must be by the sinner's own efforts and personal merit.

Second, the practical awareness that much imperfection and sin remained, despite efforts at doing penance, led to the idea of merit being transferred from very holy saints to lesser mortals.

It was claimed that this store of merit accumulated by saints and martyrs over the years could be distributed by the pope himself or through agents authorized by him. These 'indulgences', as they were called, could be bought for cash. The sale of them provided a source of income for the pope.

Third, alongside these errors with regard to human merit, there grew up the idea that the mass[4] can be, by the intention of the priest, a real sacrifice of the actual body and blood of Christ. The bread and wine were supposed to become Christ's flesh and blood. Whatever might be the value of human merit, the merit of repeated celebrations of *Christ's* death was surely inexhaustible! So the 'sacrifice of the altar' also became a source of financial gain, as masses were said (and paid for) to provide merit for the benefit of the souls of the living and the dead.

There are four ways in which the teaching of the Scriptures, and thereby of the Reformers, differed from the Roman Catholic teaching on justification:

i. *The nature of justification.* The Roman Catholic teaching was that by baptism the sinner actually receives new spiritual life, making him able to justify himself. The Reformers taught, from Scripture, that justification is the complete pardon of all sins by God's gracious decision, so that the sinner is immediately considered righteous.

ii. *The basis for justification.* The Roman Catholic teaching was that the spiritual life received in baptism was the reason for God accepting a sinner. Scripture and the Reformers taught that Christ's righteousness, being put to the sinner's account, is the only basis for justification.

iii. *The method of justification.* The Roman Catholic teaching was that the sinner is justified when the spiritual life received by baptism produces holy actions — i.e. confessions, partaking of the sacraments of the church, penances, etc. Scripture and the Reformers taught that justification is by faith in Christ alone. Such true faith will indeed produce the 'fruit of the Spirit' in the life. But justification is biblically linked to faith, not to the good works that follow belief.

iv. *The effect of justification.* The Roman Catholic teaching was that justification is never perfectly achieved. There is always need for further penance for further sin. No one can be sure of complete justification until he has reached heaven after enduring the suffering of purgatory. Scripture and the Reformers taught that justification includes the free pardon of all sin and ensures eternal life. They spoke of the Roman teaching as 'the uncertain faith, full of doubts'. This is very different from the Protestant teaching of the complete, final, irreversible nature of justification by God's gracious act.

The Roman Catholic teaching has the effect of giving importance to human effort in justification; it belittles the richness and wonder of God's grace. The merits of the life and death of Christ are no longer sufficient — the sinner must add the supposed merits of his own efforts. There is not one sacrifice only for sin; the sacrifice must be repeated endlessly in the mass. The sinner's efforts at justifying himself can have added to them the merit of other saints and martyrs. Pardon for sin is not an immediate gift of God but an uncertain thing, dependent on confession, penance and absolution granted by a human priest. And the corrupt practice of selling indulgences (which so offended Luther) arose naturally from all these errors of doctrine, as Luther so wisely saw. The biblical truth of a justification by faith freely given by God and bringing assured salvation to the sinner, flashed like an electric current through the doubts and corruptions of the sixteenth century. This new understanding led to the reforming of some churches and their renewal after the pattern of apostolic times.

Notes

[1]This term means guilt and sin which is inherited from the fall of the first man, Adam. Because all have descended from him, all share his original sin — Editor.

[2]This term means some discipline imposed in the life of the sinner to atone for venial sins that had been confessed — Editor.

47

[3]Purgatory is the name given to a supposed place of temporary suffering, after death, where those who die in favour with the church can purify their souls — Editor.

[4]The name given to the celebration of the communion service in the Roman Catholic Church — Editor.

Lecture 5: How the Roman Catholic Church thought about justification after the Reformation

In 1530 Luther and others published a statement describing how they understood the biblical teaching of the justification of sinners by God's grace alone, and by faith in the merits of Christ alone. Roman Catholic theologians rejected this doctrine as 'a novelty', meaning that it was being introduced for the first time! They appealed to earlier corrupt teachings of the Roman Church as their reason for dismissing it as a novelty.

Luther and others replied that the doctrine might be new to many in the Church of Rome because their false teachings had hidden the truth held by the apostles and the early church fathers! (See Lecture 3).

Within a few years an effort was made by Erasmus and others to try to reconcile the two opposing views of Protestant and Roman Catholic theologians.

Surprisingly, it was agreed by the Roman theologians that justification is by faith 'on account of the merits of Jesus Christ only'. However, the value of that definition depended upon what was meant by 'faith'.

For the Protestants, faith was understood as the simple act of complete reliance upon Christ, as the only hope of righteousness for sinners. For the Roman Catholic theologians, however, faith was used to mean the influence of the Holy Spirit in believers actually producing righteousness in them, and so making them acceptable to God.

> 'Sinners are justified by... faith which is a motion of the Holy Spirit whereby ... love is shed abroad in the heart and they begin to fulfil the law.'

True belief in a person's heart will be followed by growth in holiness. That person's justification does not, however, depend on that growth; it arises solely from Christ, to whom that person is united by faith. The attempt to reconcile Protestant and Roman Catholic views came to nothing. The two views of justification were quite different; one depended on the finished work of Christ for sinners; the other depended on the progressive work of the Holy Spirit in sinners.

For a long time, the Roman Catholic Church adopted a double policy against the Reformation teaching on justification. Some argued that it was a novelty unknown before; others argued that it was a biblical truth that the righteousness which justifies is that produced in the believer by God.

Many attempts have been made to try to reconcile the Protestant (Reformation) view of justification and Roman Catholic views.[1] However, no one who fully understands the Roman or the Reformed views can honestly suggest a compromise between them.

We do not deny that members of the Roman Catholic Church can ever be justified and be made acceptable to God. But we deny that sinners can ever be justified by *their own* righteousness. We reject as unbiblical the Roman teachings on justification. Those in that Church who are true believers are justified not according to the teachings of that Church but by trusting only in the merits of Christ, graciously given them by God.

Luther wrote: 'If no flesh be justified by the works of the law of God, much less shall any be justified by the rule of Benedict, Francis or Augustine... But some, finding in themselves no good works to set against the wrath and judgment of God, did fly to the death and passion of Christ, and were saved *in this simplicity*.'

Notes

[1]And there have been more since 1867, when Dr Buchanan's lectures were first published — Editor.

Lecture 6: Various Protestant views about justification after the Reformation

The unity between Reformation theologians on the subject of justification was remarkable. The biblical truth had long been hidden by the corrupt church of the 'Dark Ages'. The theological literature commonly available at that time was in error on this point. All the ceremonies and practices of the church at that time opposed the truth that justification was by faith in Christ alone. All the Reformers had been brought up in that church tradition. Yet, even though they differed in some matters, the Reformers were unanimous in their understanding of this Bible truth. All their writings, sermons, catechisms and commentaries agreed on this truth. And the fact that this truth of justification by faith alone was so often specially attacked by Roman Catholic theologians, shows that they also regarded it as the most significant of the truths brought to light at the Reformation.

In subsequent years, however, this remarkable unity

of belief in this Bible truth gave way to a variety of differing views, even among Protestants.

One of these views said that the righteousness by which sinners are justified is the righteousness of God put within believers by the life of Christ in them.

Another view was that the repentance from sin and new obedience toward God which true faith brings to the believers are the reasons for their justification.

Even more seriously in error were the views which arose among those Protestants who adopted an Antinomian theology, and among those who followed Socinianism. The former taught that Christ's merits were so given to believers that they actually became personally righteous; that believers were so united to Christ as though there were no difference between him and them; that the justification of the believer took place in eternity past, or at Christ's death, and was not related to the moment of belief on the part of the sinner; that a sense of sin or a praying for pardon were not therefore to be regarded as part of the true believer's experience.

The Socinian view, put briefly, was that God mercifully justifies those sinners who themselves repent and reform their lives. They began from the view that sin was merely a human disorder and not a crime against God involving guilt and death. Justification, therefore, was God's merciful acknowledgement of the sinner's personal efforts at self-improvement.

An attempt was made to form a compromise between the Socinian view and the Reformation teaching that justification was based only on Christ's merits. It was agreed that God could justify sinners who improved themselves by repentance and reformation. But it was suggested that God helped to influence sinners to make such self-improvement by the splendid moral example of the life and death of Christ. In this way their justification could be said to derive from Christ.

Yet another view suggested that all human beings possess an inner divine 'light' as part of their human nature. When that 'inner light' is cultivated and its guidance followed, then 'Christ is formed within'. That holy presence is the basis of the justification of that person.

Still another view suggested that by his death Christ satisfied the demands of God's justice for all mankind. The salvation of anyone would now be possible, if only there were a right response of repentance, faith and perseverance by that person.

(All these variations have one common factor that separates them from the true doctrine which was redis-covered at the Reformation. They all suggest that justi-fication — acceptance in God's sight — depends on a spiritual renewal *within* sinners and not — as the biblical doctrine asserts — on Christ's meritorious life and death *on behalf* of sinners — Editor.)

It may seem distressing that there should be so many varieties of opinion about a Bible truth. Luther suggested that such errors would arise. In every human heart there is either a readiness to boast of self-righteousness, or else a carelessness of life which is unwilling to accept any moral discipline. Either of these influences can corrupt a right understanding of justification.

The Scriptures teach that there will be division of

opinion in the Christian church: 'There must be differences of opinion among you, so that we may see who are the men of real worth' (1 Corinthians 11:19). Biblical truth has been defined because of the controversies which have arisen during all the ages of church history.

No one would deny that the work of the Holy Spirit in the believer which causes growth in holiness is inseparably connected to the work of Christ on behalf of that believer. Both are equally necessary. It is equally true that justification is not because of the former but because of the latter: by God's grace, not by human effort; by Christ's merits imputed, not by his righteousness imparted.

Lecture 7: Views about the doctrine in the Anglican Church since the Reformation

As a result of the Reformation, the Church of England held a view of justification which was completely in harmony with that of the Reformers. This is made clear by the eleventh article of the Thirty-nine Articles of the Church of England[1], for example, and by the teaching in *The Homilies*, a book of Bible teaching as officially held by the Church of England, published in 1547 and 1563 and designed to be read in all the churches.[2]

But later years saw a number of different views of justification becoming accepted within the Anglican Church. By 1628 the influence of arminian theology had caused a number of Church of England theologians to argue that justification was based on some goodness in believers and that there was no vital difference between the Roman and Protestant views.

And not only outside influences have caused a drift away from the Reformation position. There is also what has been called 'the natural popery of the human heart'. This is the willingness which is in us all to trust that there is enough good in us, in our motives, in our moral habits to recommend us to God. That permanent tendency within us is a strong influence to shift us from the old doctrine of the necessity of God's grace alone, to the teaching and practice of the Church of Rome. That 'natural popery' makes us willing to embrace any influence which seems to encourage human pride in somehow justifying ourselves!

Within the Church of England, a movement arose suggesting that our justification is to be based on the fact of Christ's incarnation and not on the perfect obedience of his life and death. By his becoming Man, they suggested, God indicated his unchangeable fatherly favour toward human beings. Another movement in the church sought to popularize again the old error[3] that we are justified by Christ 'being formed in us' or by the Holy Spirit's work in us; and went on to argue that the sacraments of the Church (not faith) are the means by which we receive this benefit.

If we understand the biblical truth, it will not be difficult to see how such teachings as these are wrong — and have been shown to be wrong many times in the past. For example, those who suggest that Christ's incarnation is the basis of justification because it shows God's fatherly love to mankind, are ignoring the fact of the sinfulness of human beings. God is not merely the Father of his creatures, he is also the Lawgiver and Judge of those creatures who are now, by their sin, rebels against him deserving his wrath. It is an error, therefore, to suggest that Christ becoming Man is a proof that human beings enjoy God's holy favour and are justified in his sight already.

Dr Newman of the Anglican Church (he later became Cardinal Newman of the Roman Church) attempted to show that both the Roman and the Protestant views of justification were correct. He suggested that both views were merely two sides of one truth; justification is by faith and it is also by human effort. Newman regarded these as separate but not opposite. He did not feel it inconsistent to hold both as true.

Looking at this variety of opinion which has arisen in the history of the Anglican Church from the Reformation until now (i.e. 1867 — Editor) it is impossible to foretell what may yet develop. What is most needed is a great spiritual revival, to bring about a return to 'the gospel of Christ; for it is the power of God unto salvation to everyone that believes; for in the gospel the righteousness of God is revealed from faith to faith, as it is written, "The just shall live by faith".' (Romans 1:16).

Notes

[1]The Article reads: 'We are accounted righteous before God, only for the merit of our Lord and Saviour Jesus Christ, by faith and not for our own works or deservings...'

[2]The Homily on Salvation includes such sentiments as:

'Christ is now the righteousness of all them that truly do believe in him.'

'This justification or righteousness which we receive of God's mercy and Christ's merits, embraced by faith, is taken, accepted and allowed of God for our perfect and full justification.'

'This doctrine … is not that our own act, to believe in Christ, or this our faith in Christ which is within us, doth justify us…'

[3]First suggested by A. Osiander (AD1550).

Part II:
Explanation of the Doctrine

Lecture 8: The meaning of the word justification as used in the Bible

To understand what a Bible word means we must examine not what the word means when used elsewhere but what it means in the Hebrew and Greek Scriptures.

Justification is used in Scripture to mean the acceptance by God of anyone as righteous. Justification means that God treats a person who is guilty of sin as not guilty; God declares that that person is to be viewed as legally righteous. (It does not mean that the person is actually made righteous, any more than 'to glorify God' can mean actually to make God glorious. The meaning is simple *to declare* that God is glorious). This use of *justification* to mean only the declaration of a person as righteous in the eyes of the law is proved in three ways;

i.   The word *justify* is used as the opposite of the word *condemn* in a number of Bible verses, e.g. Deuteronomy 25:1. To condemn the wicked does not mean actually to make them wicked, but only to declare that that is their classification in law. So 'to justify' means not to make people righteous but to declare that that is how they are to be regarded in the eyes of the law.

ii.   The words *justify* and *righteous* are most often used in verses which speak about some legal or judicial act. Examples of such Scriptures are: Psalm 32:1; 143:2; Romans 8:33. These are references to justification as part of a judicial process. This confirms that to justify a person in Bible usage means to declare that person legally righteous.

iii. Other words or phrases used as equivalent to justification also indicate a change of legal relationship and not a change of character. For example, justification is described as 'the imputation of righteousness' (Romans 4:3,6-8; 2 Corinthians 5:19, 21). This means (Romans 4:5) that righteousness is reckoned to belong to a person who is in fact ungodly.[1] Thus justification is again shown to be a legal declaration graciously made by God reckoning the sinner to be pardoned of sin and regarded as righteous by having Christ's merit.

Justification has two parts: it means the acceptance by God of sinners as righteous: and it also means the experience of assurance when sinners know that they are justified. There is the fact of justification and there is the evidence of that fact. One is God's declaration; the other is a person's awareness of the fact. Clearly, God's decision to justify someone must precede any evidence

64

of justification in that person.

The difference between these two 'faces' of justification can be illustrated by what will happen at the final judgment. All those whom God has justified will then be seen publicly by all to be justified ones (Matthew 25:32). That day is called in Scripture the day of 'the revelation of the sons of God' (Romans 8:19).

These two parts of justification, the fact and the evidence of it, account for the apparent contradiction between Paul and James, who both wrote about justification. Paul says that we are 'justified by faith without the deeds of the law' (Romans 3:28). James says 'by works a man is justified, not by faith only' (James 2:24). There is no contradiction here. Paul is speaking of *the fact* of justification. Sinners are justified because God graciously pardons and accepts them for Christ's sake and not because of any deeds of theirs. This justification is received by faith alone.

James, however, is writing of a person's *awareness* of being justified. People have no reason to suppose they are justified unless their deeds give holy proof of the fact. Paul writes of God's declaration of justification: it does not depend on our good deeds. James writes of how it may be known that people are justified: holy living is the evidence of it.

Both Paul and James give Abraham as an example of their arguments. Both parts of justification can be seen in Abraham. First, he was justified by faith before he was circumcised. Second, there was great evidence of his justification in his life, for he did not hesitate to obey God's commands to him.

Paul was writing against the idea that we can justify

ourselves in God's sight by our human efforts. James was writing against the teaching that it does not matter how believers live. Justification is by the gracious gift of God and is made evident by the holy lives of believers. Both of these truths are included in what is meant by justification.

Notes

[1]Believers will not remain ungodly if they are justified but will begin to show marks of new spiritual life. But they can be declared pardoned and justified even though ungodly at the moment of conversion — Editor.

Lecture 9: What justification is

Justification can be thought of in two ways: it is something God does; it is something sinners receive. In both cases it includes: the full pardon of sin; the entrance into God's favour; and the right to eternal life.

i.   Justification is something God does. 'God is the one who justifies' (Romans 8:33). We understand therefore that justification is something that takes place outside of us. God's purposes of salvation were formed before the world began, so they must be independent of our influence. Also, justification is an act which is completed at once — there is no such thing as progressive justification; it is an act of lasting value. Justified sinners are united to Christ for ever (John 5:24).

   Yet this justification is not merely something that God did in eternity past and now reveals, but an act of God concerning particular individuals which takes place at a certain time in their lives. Until sinners believe, they are under God's wrath (John 3:36). When by God's grace they are rescued and pardoned, their relationship with God is altered from that moment. In other words, they are justified!

ii. Justification is something sinners receive. It includes full pardon, God's favour, and eternal life (John 3:16). Yet there are some people — Roman Catholic and Protestant alike — who have denied that justification includes a *complete* pardon from sin. Some have suggested that the pardon relates only to that sinfulness which we inherit; others that it relates to the sins committed before conversion; and others that it relates to the dominion of sin over believers. It is said that believers by their own effort must still earn remission from the punishment due for the sins they commit. All these errors arise from ignorance or unbelief about the true nature of sin and God's wrath on it.

Pardon is not properly understood until it is realized that sin brings guilt and guilt remains for ever. Repentance, even regeneration, cannot alter the fact of past guilt. Only pardon can remove guilt. It cannot be right, therefore, to suggest that our justification means the pardon only of some aspect of our sin. Pardon removes *all* guilt, and is the only thing that can. If guilt remains, there has not been real pardon.

Nor is it true that justification means merely our being pardoned for the past, as though we must thereafter earn our acceptance by God. The pardon of sin does restore the sinner to a state of innocence.

However, we are required not merely to be innocent before God, but to be positively righteous, and Scripture clearly teaches that God does impute such a righteousness (Romans 4:6). Our possessing the positive merits of Christ by faith is a part of our justification, as much as is our pardon.

The Christian privileges received by justified believers rise in an ascending scale of glory. There is pardon crowned by righteousness; righteousness crowned by acceptance with God; acceptance crowned by adoption as children and heirs of God!

iii. Justification and sanctification are inseparably connected but they differ from each other. In justification, God *imputes* the righteousness of Christ to believers; in sanctification, the Holy Spirit *imparts* the grace of holiness and gives strength to live righteously. In justification, sin is pardoned; in sanctification, sin is actually subdued. Justification frees all believers equally from the wrath of God; sanctification is never equal in all believers but varies as each believer grows in grace. Sanctification is never perfect in any person in this life but believers can never be more justified than they are now! Their justification already includes the fullest acceptance with God and the right to eternal life.

Lecture 10:Justification and God's law

Most of the wrong ideas about justification have arisen because of wrong ideas about the law of God. By the law of God we mean the moral rules by which he governs his creation. If the justice of God did not require our strict obedience to his laws, or if God's mercy could somehow excuse our disobedience to his laws, then being justified in the sight of God would be an easy matter! We would not have to keep his laws perfectly.

The truth is that God's law requires our perfect obedience: no one can be justified in God's sight unless completely righteous, i.e. without fault, and perfectly holy. The strictness of God's justice makes it impossible for him to relax the requirements for justification. We must understand that God's law is the high standard our righteousness must reach if we are to be justified.

This is clearly seen in the arrangement that God made with Adam and Eve when they were first created. God gave them a special command. Obedience brought the reward of continued life; disobedience brought them the penalty of death. Their justification depended solely on their perfect obedience to that law.

Moreover, Scripture reveals that Adam was required to obey God perfectly, not merely for his own sake but also as the representative of every human person who would descend from him (Romans 5:12). There is no satisfactory explanation for the universal presence of sin in the human race nor of the universality of death unless we accept the Bible record that these were the results of Adam's sin, now affecting us all.

It follows from this that Adam's sin has made us all sinners. As our representative, his guilt is reckoned ours. Yet this is not our only guilt. We also inherit Adam's sinful nature and this causes us to sin. We add our own guilt to the guilt we receive from Adam! So for two reasons — Adam's guilt and our own guilt — we cannot justify ourselves by claiming to have kept God's law without fault. There is something 'the law cannot do' (Romans 8:3): it cannot justify sinners, and we are doubly such. We are therefore by ourselves utterly beyond justification.

To escape this difficulty some have suggested that God's law no longer has to be obeyed, or they suggest that the law has been so modified as to make obedience to it a possibility, even by sinners. (A third possibility, that people are not sinners and therefore are well able to keep God's law, is obviously so far from the truth as not to require serious discussion).

Can we say that God's law has been cancelled and no longer needs to be obeyed? No! if God does not command our obedience any more, we are no longer controlled by any moral government at all. If our Maker gives us no rules, sin has no meaning. 'Sin is not imputed when there is no law' (Romans 5:13). The voice of conscience is an illusion if there are no universal rules. It is better to be governed by a God who is righteous than to live in a world that is lawless.

Then if the law of God is not cancelled, can we say that it has been modified to make it possible for sinners to keep it? If we say so, then human inability to keep God's law means that the law must be adjusted to suit human weakness. But this would mean that the more wicked a person becomes, the more God's law must be relaxed, and God's law would be diminished by increasing sin!

Others say that the suffering and death of Christ have modified what behaviour God now requires of us, so that if we are sincerely trying to live our best, we can be justified, though we are imperfect. But many questions then arise, e.g. What is this new, modified law? Can any law, even a modified one, be satisfied with *imperfect* obedience? If imperfection is permissible, what is the minimum amount of obedience possible? How can imperfect obedience be sincere if it is known to be imperfect? Where is it said in Scripture that Christ came to modify the law?

No Christians are perfect beings, yet they are acceptable to God despite imperfect obedience. But they are not accepted for themselves but only through their relationship to Jesus Christ. Believers do not rely on their own imperfect acts for righteousness but on the merit of Jesus Christ.

Finally, it must be understood that the laws of God

are not merely rules he has devised which he can, if he wishes, cancel or modify. God's laws are an expression of his own moral nature. He is holy, just and good. Therefore his laws are holy, just and good. His law can never command anything less than holiness, justice and goodness. God's law cannot be cancelled or modified unless his nature can also be altered...

It follows from this that God cannot be merciful to any guilty person unless in some way atonement has been made for that person's sin. God's holiness, justice and goodness must be satisfied before anyone can be justified. The law must be fulfilled. At this point we receive the gospel with joy, for it is the only way in which sinners may be justified.

Lecture 11:Justification and the life and death of Christ

Justification and the coming of Christ are both shown in Scripture to be related to God's law. The demands of God's law provide the need for us to be justified; Christ came to fulfil that law. Justification and the coming of Christ must therefore be related to each other. All Christians will agree that Christ obeyed all God's will and that our justification arises from that obedience. Not all are agreed, however, as to exactly how our justification arises from Christ's obedience.

Some have suggested that the obedience of Christ is the cause of God's love toward sinners. Others suggest that because he is love, God can be gracious to sinners and not require their sins to be atoned for, as though God's love makes it impossible for him also to be angry against sin. Scripture shows both of these views to be wrong, in the following ways:

i.   Scripture makes it clear that it was God's eternal purpose to justify the ungodly through Christ and by this to reveal the perfection of his own divine nature. For example, we read in Scripture about God's 'eternal purpose, which he purposed in Christ Jesus our Lord' (Ephesians 3:11). Christ's obedience to God's law was not, therefore, the cause of God's love to sinners. Instead, it was God's eternal love which formed the purpose of sending Christ to keep his law and to die for sinners. Our salvation reveals God's nature to be love.

Moreover, God's plan of salvation reveals the fact that God is a Trinity. The Scriptures teach that God the Father sent God the Son to be the Saviour and that God the Holy Spirit applies that salvation to sinners. Scripture clearly shows that these three divine Persons agreed together to carry out the plan of salvation. Believers may comfort themselves that salvation rests on the united, eternal purpose of a Triune God. Salvation reveals God's Triune nature.

Scripture also makes it clear that God can experience love and holy wrath together. Was anyone so loved by God the Father as the Son? Yet did anyone so suffer holy wrath on sin as Christ on the cross? So, in the justification of sinners, God's love is satisfied. Sinners are saved by Christ's death for them, and God's holy wrath is satisfied. Sin is atoned for by Christ's death. God displays the eternal perfections of his justice and his love in the plan of salvation in a way not seen anywhere else.

ii. Scripture reveals that Christ saves and justifies his people by becoming a substitute for them. He is not merely a prophet, to teach them; not merely a king, to govern them; Christ is a priest and a sacrifice, a representative of his people.

Some have doubted that one person can in this way justly take the punishment due to another. They argue that the one who sins must be punished. The answer is that by making Adam the representative of the human race, God has already used the method of one taking the place of others (Romans 5:19). If God has used this method of representation, it must be a right method. Therefore, just as the welfare of many depended on Adam, so also the welfare of many depends on Christ.

In order that Christ should be a true substitute, he was 'made of a woman, made under the law' (Galatians 4:4). In other words, he had the same human nature as his people and was to keep the same law that his people had failed to keep. Because of these similarities, Christ was acceptable as a legal substitute for his people.

iii. Scripture says that Christ's work as the Saviour consisted of his incarnation, his life of complete obedience to the Father, and his sufferings and death (Philippians 2:8). The union of human and divine natures in Christ is the unique qualification which makes him so fit for the work of mediator between God and mankind. Only God could satisfy an offended God. That might seem impossible. If all the sinners in the world contributed together, their total sacrifice would be inadequate. But in Christ, the divine and human natures are so joined that a perfect Man can be the sacrifice, possessing also the infinite worth of God's nature. In other words, the incarnation of Christ made possible all the excellence of his work as mediator.

This work included being the perfect servant of God throughout his life and being the substitute for his people in his death. Christ was thus the one perfect mediator between God and mankind. Various causes contributed to his death — the will of God, his own willingness, his love, the wickedness of the people who hated him, the work of Satan, etc. But the one great reason for his death was the sins of his people (Isaiah 53:5). God's law required the punishment of sin and the righteousness of obedience. In Christ, both were fulfilled; not on his own account, but on behalf of others.

iv. Scripture tells us that what Christ has done completely satisfied God's law. Christ obeyed *all* the requirements of the law and paid *all* the penalties of the law. Therefore he actually obtained the salvation of all for whom he died; the law has no more hold over them.

Some people have suggested that the merits of Christ's work can only be obtained by sinners now doing good works themselves. Such a view not only prevents us from receiving a full salvation at once, but also insults Christ by dishonouring his work. (We will look at this matter more fully in the next chapter). On the contrary, we understand from Scripture that, as a result of the excellence of his saving work, Christ now has 'all power in heaven and earth' to give eternal life to those whom he chooses. So what need is there of any additional merit from us?

v. The justification of sinners is possible, according to Scripture, because Christ has satisfied God's law and justice. God has not merely cancelled the punishment of sin, nor has he ignored the requirements of his justice. To have done so would have made his justice unimportant. In fact, God's justice has been honoured because Christ fully satisfied God's demands.

To summarise the above, justification is based on the death of Christ (Romans 5:9,10). It is linked to Christ's obedience (Hebrews 5:8); to his righteousness (Isaiah 45:24-25); to his name (1 Corinthians 6:11); to his knowledge (John 17:3-4). Christ's people are absolutely dependent for their acceptance with God on the excellence of all aspects of Christ's work. See Jeremiah 23:6.

In such a display of Christ's abilities as this, we can see again how the plan of salvation reveals different aspects of the glorious nature of God. The glory of God is seen in the face of Jesus Christ. Our justification, then, arises from God's eternal intention to display his own glory in our salvation. What a comfort to us to have this assurance and to know that all God's will is now honoured and fully satisfied on our behalf!

Lecture 12: Christ's merits are the only ground for our justification

Many agree that our justification is related to the work of Christ as Saviour and Mediator. But they do not all agree that justification depends on Christ's work *alone*. As we have seen in the previous chapter, some suggest that what Christ has done does not actually justify anyone, but simply makes it possible for us now to be justified if we add our own good works to Christ's work. It is therefore necessary for us to be quite sure that the righteousness of Christ is the only basis for our justification. Scripture teaches that it is so; I offer four points:

i.   The righteousness on which justification depends is variously described as 'the righteousness *of Christ*'; 'the righteousness *which is by faith*'; 'the obedience *of One*', etc. Most importantly, it is called 'the righteousness *of God*'. From these phrases it is clear that no righteousness contributed by saved or unsaved persons is included in the description of their justification.

If our righteousness could make us acceptable to God, then surely the 'righteousness *of God*' would not be necessary. If the 'righteousness *of God*' is what is needed (as Scripture teaches), then no human righteousness is of any use; see Romans 3:20-22. Scripture makes clear that justification rests on the 'righteousness *of God*'. The Bible never suggests that human righteousness is necessary for our acceptance with God.

But what is meant by the phrase 'righteousness of God'? Some have suggested that the meaning is merely God's *method* of justifying sinners. In that case, God's righteousness would not mean actual merit that can be transferred to others. But this interpretation will not satisfy such verses as: 'Christ is made of God... righteousness to us' (1 Corinthians 1:30). The meaning of this must be that the merits of Christ's righteous life and obedient death are actually given to us. So the 'righteousness of God' cannot mean merely God's method of making us righteous but must mean *the value of right things done by God in Christ*.

Other descriptions of this righteousness, such as 'the righteousness *of Christ*', or 'the obedience *of One*', also confirm that the righteousness on which justification depends is not some divine method of working but is the *actual merit* obtained by Christ through his life and death.

ii. Believers are justified by the value of this righteousness being put to their credit. Justification does not, however, make them personally righteous characters. For example, the wrong done by Onesimus against Philemon was to be put to Paul's account (Philemon 18). But the wrong was not actually done by Paul. It was still Onesimus who was guilty of sin. In the same way, Christ's righteousness being put to our account does not mean that we thereby can be said to have performed these meritorious acts.

Similarly, our sins were truly reckoned to Christ when he died in our place. Yet it is never said that he committed those sins. So when his righteousness is reckoned to us, it is not meant that we have actually lived righteously.

iii. Even when the righteousness of Christ is credited to any sinner, it remains *Christ's* righteousness. This righteousness is shared with the sinner, certainly, but it never ceases to belong to Christ. The sinner can never say, 'I am now able to claim eternal life as a reward because I am myself righteous'. Righteousness is only ours by our being united to Christ. Our righteousness is 'in him'.

iv. All that Christ did in perfectly obeying his Father's will and in giving himself on the cross, he did as *the substitute for his people*. To them is given, therefore, the whole merit that Christ obtained. The justification that sinners receive is full and complete. They need nothing more to complete their acceptance with God.

Some have suggested that this doctrine of imputation, as it is called (imputation means the credit of

81

good, or evil, transferred, as it were, from one person to another), is a theory invented by human beings. They do not believe, therefore, that all are made sinners because of Adam's sin; nor do they believe that any are made righteous solely because of Christ's obedience. Against this, it must be said that the imputation of sin and of righteousness is a fact revealed in Scripture, as we have already seen in previous chapters. What God has revealed in Scripture is to be believed by us: 'In the Lord have I righteousness and strength; even to him shall men come... in the Lord shall all the seed of Israel be justified and shall glory' (Isaiah 45:24-25). There is no righteousness for us in any other way than by Christ's righteousness being reckoned as ours.

Lecture 13:Justification as related to God's grace and human effort

Some have suggested that if our justification is a gift to us by God's grace, it cannot be the result of a redemption paid. But Paul has no difficulty in linking both God's grace and Christ's redemptive work with our justification: we are 'justified freely by his grace through the redemption which is in Christ Jesus' (Romans 3:24).

We must not think of God's grace to us as one of the things procured by the redemptive work of Christ. Rather, the redemptive work of Christ flows out of God's grace to us. Justification therefore is by grace and through the redemption paid by Christ.

Justification by God's gracious gift is always linked in Scripture with faith and grace and never with any acts sinners can do (Romans 4:16). On the contrary, Paul draws a strong contrast between attempts at justification by human effort and a justification received 'by the faith of Christ' (Galatians 2:16). Clearly, biblical justification is related to grace and faith, and not to human works.

We can easily see why sinners cannot be justified by

their own efforts. They are already guilty because they have sinned. There is therefore no way they can, as guilty people, offer good works! God's law has to condemn them as guilty; it cannot call them righteous, or approve of their works.

Some have argued that the only law that has to be kept to earn justification in God's sight is the outward ceremonial law given to the Jews. If so, it is conceivable that a person could keep it. However, whenever Paul writes of the law that must be perfectly kept — and which, therefore, can never justify guilty sinners — he clearly refers not to any ceremonial acts but to the universal and moral law of God (Romans 3:10-20).

Moreover, when Paul writes of Abraham being justified, he indicates that this was before the ceremony of circumcision was introduced (Romans 4:3; compare Genesis 15:6. Circumcision was not required until Genesis 17). Clearly, Abraham was not justified by keeping any ceremonial law. So we cannot agree that righteousness is merely a matter of observing outward ceremonies.

God requires his moral law to be kept perfectly. Therefore, as far as guilty sinners are concerned, 'by the deeds of the law shall no flesh be justified in his sight'. Good works cannot be done by the guilty. To be described as 'good' in God's sight, an action must:

    i.   Conform to his will
   ii.   be done out of obedience
  iii.   spring from a right motive
  iv.   be an expression of love to God
   v.   result in God's glory

So justification can never be possible if it has to be by the efforts of guilty sinners, who could never perform a single 'good' work that fulfils these five requirements.

Even in the case of believers, justification is not based on any of their good works. Believers certainly are to do good works (Hebrews 13:15,16), which are the effects of their faith, as is clearly shown by the examples of Hebrews 11. These good works, the effects of faith, are the evidence of justification — which, we have seen, is by faith. (We will study this in detail in the next chapter). The good works of believers cannot be the *reason* for justification if they are the *evidence* of it having happened!

Moreover, even the good works of believers lack perfection (Galatians 5:17). Although the good works of believers are more pleasing to God than the wicked works of the ungodly, they are still not perfect, for no believers are spiritually perfect in this life. Indeed, the greater the extent to which believers grow spiritually mature, the more they appreciate how serious their sins are. So even the good works of believers are not good enough to earn their justification.

Justification by grace and faith does not deny the need for believers to display the good fruit of the Spirit in their lives, but it does deny that those good works are the reason for the justification of believers (Philippians 3:7-9).

Lecture 14: Justification as related to faith

Some have suggested that although we cannot obtain justification by any acts we perform, yet faith itself is a meritorious act which, to some extent, makes our justification possible. Concerning Abraham, the Bible says that his faith 'was counted to him for righteousness' (Romans 4:3). Some suggest therefore that Abraham's faith was the reason for his being justified, and that the possession of faith *is the same thing* as justification.

Righteousness is variously described in Scripture as being 'of faith', 'to faith', 'by faith' and 'through faith'. Obviously there is a close connection between justification and faith; but it is just as obvious that they cannot be two names for the same thing if the two things have to be related by these prepositions 'of', 'to', 'by' and 'through'.

How then are we to understand the verse 'Abraham believed God and it (i.e. his faith) was counted to him for righteousness'? There are two ways in which this statement has been understood.

i.   The word 'faith' is often used to mean not the act of believing but the truths believed, e.g. 'the faith once delivered to the saints' (Jude 3). If the word 'faith' is used of Abraham in this sense, then it means that it was Christ (the promised Seed) that was counted to Abraham for righteousness, because the promise of the Seed was the truth that Abraham believed (Genesis 15:5,6).

ii. Others have suggested that the term 'faith' is to be understood as meaning Abraham's act of believing. God could see that this faith was a genuine saving faith. It was therefore a faith that God knew would attain to righteousness; it would cause Abraham to be obedient to God. As a seed has a potential fruit in it, so this faith bore within it the certainty of a full salvation for Abraham; he was therefore regarded as justified.

The phrase used of Abraham's faith, 'for righteousness' or 'as righteousness' — is, in Romans 4:3, literally '*toward* righteousness'. It is clear from this that justification and faith, while closely related, are not the same. Faith is not the same as the righteousness which provides justification; but faith 'looks toward' that justification.

Faith is described as God's gift (Philippians 1:29). And this faith is a spiritual grace which produces obedience to God's will in our lives. Yet, as we have seen, this obedience of faith is not the righteousness by means of which we are accepted by God. Obedient faith is *the means by which we receive* Christ's righteousness. Faith is the instrument by which righteousness is procured. Eating is necessary for the nourishment of our bodies, but it is the food we eat which actually nourishes us. Likewise, faith is necessary to receive righteousness but it is the righteousness of Christ which actually justifies us.

Faith is the only means for the receiving of justification. Justification is not by faith *plus* the knowledge that one is among the elect of God. Justification is not by faith *plus* a certain amount of conviction of sin. True, none will believe unless they are the elect of God and are convicted of their sin and need of a Saviour. But it is primarily our faith in God's promise of salvation in Christ for sinners which brings justification, not anything else we may know or feel.

The reason why faith alone is the instrument by which we receive justification is that it is by believing — and in no other way — that we can rely on Christ's saving work. It is not sorrow for sin that unites us to Christ. It is not the spiritual graces of love and hope which make us partakers of Christ's righteousness. It is by the use of faith that sinners rely on Christ for salvation.

Other graces are present whenever true faith is present because faith is part of the whole spiritual life newly present in believers by the Holy Spirit's work. But it is particularly faith which is connected to justification more directly than any other grace.

Lecture 15: Justification and the work of the Holy Spirit

The spiritual change in the life of the believer which is called 'a new creation' (2 Corinthians 5:17) is the work of the Holy Spirit. It is an error, however, to suggest that justification depends on this work of the Spirit *in* the sinner. Justification, as we have already seen, depends on the life and death of Christ *for* the sinner.

It is important not to confuse these two divine activities. Because justification depends on the work of Christ which is now finished, our justification is as complete as it ever can be. If it depended on the continuing work of the Spirit in us, our justification would still be very incomplete because the Spirit's work in us is as yet incomplete.

The three Persons in the Triune God agree together in the purpose of salvation for sinners. Yet Scripture also indicates that each of the divine Persons takes a lead in carrying out different parts of that plan. The Father is described as loving the redeemed and as sending the Son to be their Saviour. The Son is described as coming to do the Father's will and bearing our sins in his own body. The Spirit is described as sent by the Son from the Father to bear witness of Christ, to convince of sin and to dwell in believers.

We must therefore distinguish between what Christ has done for us and what the Spirit does in us. And justification arises from the work of Christ for sinners, as we have previously seen.

The Spirit's work is as necessary for our salvation as is the work of Christ (1 Corinthians 6:11). But the two works serve different purposes. The work of Christ reconciles us to God by removing our guilt and giving us a new righteousness. The work of the Spirit is actually to change our wills and cause us to trust and to follow Christ. (Left to ourselves we — being dead in sin — would never turn to Christ). Christ procured our salvation. The Spirit applies that salvation to us. The work of the Spirit is to bear witness to Christ (John 15:26). The work of the Spirit therefore is not the cause of our redemption but the consequence of a redemption already procured by Christ; it is the evidence of, and not the reason for, our justification.

While it is true that the work of Christ and the work of the Spirit differ in their particular purposes, they must not be isolated one from the other. No one who is justified can fail to be renewed; no one who is renewed can fail to be justified. There comes a point, whether consciously or not, in the life of every true convert of 'passing from death to life'. At that point, the believer's justification and regeneration are coincident in time.

The Spirit has applied the merit of the work of Christ to the sinner and at the same time produced in that sinner a new trust and love for Christ.

If it is asked, 'How can a holy God give his Spirit to a sinner still in sin?', or 'How can God justify a sinner to whom the Spirit has not yet applied the merits of Christ? Which comes first?', we can only answer by remembering that God's purposes of mercy toward his elect are eternal. It was always his purpose to justify and regenerate them. So *both* justification and regeneration are gifts of the same eternal grace. Both of them originate in God's eternal purposes. Neither of them, therefore, is of greater priority than its companion.

Conclusions

Conclusions

1. We need to understand that this Bible doctrine of justification is one of the glories of the Christian gospel. In no other faith is there such an adequate solution to the problem of how a holy God can justify sinners without either making little of sin or denying the greatness of God's holiness. By this doctrine, sin is fully atoned for; God's holiness is fully satisfied; and yet sinners are saved!

2. We need to realize that there are basically only two kinds of religion. There is the religion which teaches that our justification is essentially and absolutely the free gift of God through the righteousness of Christ alone, received by faith. This is the religion of the Bible.

    There is also the religion which suggests that our justification depends on our personal holiness and obedience to God. This, we argue, is contrary to the biblical teaching and is therefore false religion. From the earliest period of the Christian church, there has been this division between saving truth and unbiblical error (Galatians 1:3-7).

Surely it is our duty to discover what is the truth as revealed by God in the Scripture. It is a matter of supreme importance to comply with the way of salvation which God has shown. Not to have faith in God's way of salvation, whether because of carelessness or hatred of the truth, is to be guilty of the great sin of unbelief — perhaps even fatally so.